FOLLOW ME

POCKET DEVOTIONS FOR LENT 2003

GABE HUCK

Augsburg Fortress
Minneapolis

Follow Me: Pocket Devotions for Lent 2003
Copyright © 2002 Augsburg Fortress. All rights reserved. Except for brief quotations in critical articles or reviews, no part of this book may be reproduced in any manner without prior written permission from the publisher. Write to: Permissions, Augsburg Fortress, Box 1209, Minneapolis, MN 55440-1209.
Or visit www.augsburgfortress.org/copyrights

Scripture quotations, unless otherwise noted, are from the New Revised Standard Version (NRSV) Bible, copyright © 1989 Division of Christian Education of the National Council of Churches of Christ in the United States of America. Used by permission.

Most readings are from *Between Sundays: Daily Bible Readings* (ISBN 0-8066-3590-8).

"Mother of God" reprinted with the permission of Scribner, an imprint of Simon & Schuster Adult Publishing Group, from *The Collected Works of W.B. Yeats,* Vol. 1: *The Poems, Revised,* ed. Richard J. Finneran. Copyright © 1933 by The Macmillan Company; copyright renewed © 1961 by Bertha Georgie Yeats.

Cover photography: © The Crosiers. Used by permission.
Cover design: David Meyer
Interior design: Marti Naughton
Editors: Robert Buckley Farlee and Becky Lowe

Manufactured in the USA.
09 08 07 06 05 04 03 02

ISBN 0-8066-3408-1
1 2 3 4 5 6 7 8 9 10

ASH WEDNESDAY, MARCH 5, 2003

*You shall be called the repairer of the breach, the
restorer of streets to live in.*   ISAIAH 58:12

THE DAY IS NAMED FOR ASHES; the season is named for the
hard and humiliating process called spring, the struggle
for life. It is Ash Wednesday. It is Lent. The church puts on
ashes and earth, dust and ashes—God's gifts but hard to take.

Start from where we are, start with who we are. That is the
summons we receive today. This is not a polite invitation to
join in a nondescript sort of Lent. It is a command, a summons—think of it as coming from the one who is throwing a
wedding feast and is furious that the originally invited guests
didn't show up. Nothing of Lent says that "the pleasure of
your company is requested." Rather, the word of Ash Wednesday is: "Get yourself in here now!"

In where? What sort of a place is Lent? Lent has its own
evolutions in the various Christian churches, but it holds to
this: It will end at the font. It will end when, ready or not, we
hear the scriptures and do the deeds that prepare us to go to
the waters of baptism and to renew fidelity to our own baptism. It will end in the passover, the mystery at the heart of
things for us: that in Christ God was reconciling the world,
that in the cross of Jesus life and death did battle and life was
victorious. And so in the waters of baptism once and always
we died to live in Christ. And it is all *we*. Each of us takes up
Lent, but the church—the baptized and those now chosen for
baptism—*does* Lent.

On this first day, then, we have Isaiah giving us all a rather
puzzling name: repairer of the breach, restorer of streets to
live in. What a wonder it is, this chapter 58 of Isaiah. And
what a wonder it is that the church can call us to Lent's fasting
and at the same time let Isaiah tell us what fasting truly means.
"Look," this is God's word to Isaiah, "you fast only to quarrel
and to fight and to strike with a wicked fist" (v. 4). Then come
those words that will ever challenge us: "Is not this the fast
that I choose: to loose the bonds of injustice . . . to let the oppressed go free, and to break every yoke? Is it not to share
your bread with the hungry, and bring the homeless poor into

your house?" (v. 6-7). Repair what is broken, and make the streets once again places for human community.

The fasting we do in Lent—will it lead us to violence or to justice? The question is as simple and as hard as that.

> *God, you demand our presence. You call us to keep Lent with all its beauty and rigor. Lead us to that fast that feeds the hungry and makes this world a watered garden. In mercy hear us.*

THURSDAY, MARCH 6, 2003

I turned to the Lord God, to seek an answer by prayer and supplication with fasting and sackcloth and ashes. DANIEL 9:3

THE RETURN TO THE FONT, the work of Lent each year, is not unlike this story of Daniel. There is something amiss, something not right, says Daniel. He didn't have to see it that way. Times weren't that bad in Babylon. Go along to get along. This was quite a lovely place, really, and even those from far-off conquered peoples could do well.

But here is Daniel in the ashes. Here is well-off Daniel fasting from all the good things around him. He is trying to still the noises and hear what the Lord might be saying. He is trying to get away from the business and the plenty and the ample distractions and for once truly see. See what? We can say, "see what matters most," but it isn't so simple. Maybe it is a matter of fasting and ashes to clear the sight, clear the ears, clear the hours and the affections and bring to words, bring to light, something as wondrous as the truth. So he fasts. So he prays.

And so might we. Sometimes our devotion and prayer is spontaneous, but the church doesn't depend on the spontaneous or most of us might never get there. Instead, we come round to Lent and we study to be something like Daniel. We figure out: What in our life—as a church, a household, an individual—is keeping our ears from hearing? What in our life—church, household, individual—is keeping our eyes from seeing? Hearing what? Seeing what?

That is of course the problem. We figure it out by beginning to clear the decks. We will figure out the fast, figure out what could go—what as a household or as an individual is selling us short, wasting our time, coddling us, distracting us from being the people who went down into baptism's waters and came out alive in Christ Jesus the Lord. The Daniel in each of us stands here ready to say: I can do without a good deal that I've been told I need. I need ears ready to hear the prophets and gospel straight; I need eyes ready to see who needs me; I need time, not for the distractions of TV or gadgets, but for those very ones who need me. Lent can turn life around. What else would it be for?

> *Lord God, keeping covenant and steadfast love with those who love you and keep your commandments, we have sinned and done wrong, acted wickedly and rebelled. We have not listened to your servants the prophets. Have mercy, Lord, and in mercy hear us.*

FRIDAY, MARCH 7, 2003

> *We do not present our supplication before you on the ground of our righteousness, but on the ground of your great mercies. O Lord, hear; O Lord, forgive; O Lord, listen and act and do not delay!*   DANIEL 9:18-19

ONE THING THAT THE PEOPLES of the book—Jews, Christians, Muslims—have all tried to do is make supplication to God. All we have to do is open the book of Psalms to learn how deep and how vast is this kind of praying for Jews and, through them, for Christians. There was a time in the church when those to be baptized at Easter were sent out of the assembly every Lord's day because they were not yet allowed to take part in the eucharist, nor to take part in the greeting of peace, nor to take part in the great prayers of supplication.

Only those baptized could do these deeds. But we must understand that doing these deeds was not simply a right received in baptism, it was understood to be a responsibility, a duty, an obligation received in baptism.

Daniel fasts and he prays. So do we in Lent. These two habits go together. The discipline of fasting has many dimensions. We may fast from food or kinds of food, from disrespect for food and disrespect for the hungry. We may fast from some of the ways that our culture of consuming wants us to live, ways that often leave us exhausted, oblivious of what makes for a peace-filled life. We may fast from the thousands of images that television and other media throw at us, images that rob us of the time and the spirit and the will to imagine how anything other than greed and violence can be the human lot.

Then we can bring some energy to supplication. We can daily at home and Sunday in our assembly lift up to God all that is so in need of mercy and grace, love and forgiveness. We can have on our lips the names of those who are sick and those who mourn their dead. We can name the people who are being pushed around, imprisoned, made refugees and exiles by the acts of governments—ours included—and other powers. We can name our children and our elders, demanding God's attention for them in their hard or vulnerable times. We can clamor for God's mercy on ourselves.

A rhythm will come, a rhythm made of life and prayer. We begin to understand: This is what the baptized people do, we who love the world in all its trouble. We go down on our knees or we stand on our feet and we make a racket. We do not cease to clamor before God on behalf of all, we are the voice for all who suffer in this world and the voice even of the earth itself. That is simply what we do, because of God's great mercies.

> *Incline your ear, O my God, and hear. Open your eyes and look at our desolation. O Lord, hear! O Lord, forgive! O Lord, listen and act and do not delay! (from Daniel 9:18-19)*

SATURDAY, MARCH 8, 2003

Then I acknowledged my sin to you, and I did not hide my iniquity; I said, "I will confess my transgressions to the LORD," and you forgave the guilt of my sin. PSALM 32:5

HAS THE WORLD AWAKENED to forgiveness? To asking for forgiveness? For Christians there is no prayer more familiar than "forgive us as we forgive." But in recent years even governments, speaking for their people, have asked forgiveness of other peoples, of indigenous people, of other nations. Church bodies have done the same, recognizing that they have played a part in evil done to Jews and to Muslims, to people of color, to women, to children.

But among those who have been wronged is there evidence of forgiveness? Often, of course, that cannot be answered, for those wronged are dead. The native peoples, those who died in gas chambers and killing fields, those who were enslaved and raped and brutalized: they are so many millions among the dead. And when we ponder the evil done to them, done to the innocent—as long ago as Cain and Abel, as recently as this morning's paper—can we believe in forgiveness? When we allow ourselves to come closer, even for a moment, so that we begin to think of ourselves in their places—arrested and imprisoned without cause, a child abandoned by family and community, a woman beaten over and over again, a child dead of bad water in a world that knows how to make water drinkable—what do we know of forgiveness?

But some of us do know something. And all of us know some who know something. And all of us can see, if only here and there, individual examples of those who have forgiven. And we are amazed at this, not certain we could do it or want to do it. It is fine to apologize, humbling but acceptable. But to forgive? "Evil will be punished" says a post-September 11 T-shirt. We who keep Lent believe: Evil can be forgiven. It cannot be stamped out by punishment, not ever. It can be forgiven. And then what might happen?

Psalm 32 ponders the way we waste away when we

7

seek forgiveness and the healing we experience when forgiven. Where in the world shall we start?

> *Dear God, in the time of distress, keep safe all your cherished world. From all the evil we have done to one another, deliver us through the wonder and grace of your forgiveness and our own.*

FIRST SUNDAY IN LENT, MARCH 9, 2003

> *The Spirit immediately drove [Jesus] out into the wilderness. He was in the wilderness forty days, tempted by Satan; and he was with the wild beasts; and the angels waited on him.* MARK 1:12-13

HERE IN MARK'S TERSE VERSION is one way to think about this Lent we have begun. Every word is a chamber filled with stories already known, and those stories give us ears to hear this new story and indeed to take our part in it.

What is this Spirit that drives Jesus? Is this something like what happened when the spirit of the Lord came on Gideon and on Jephthah, and on Samson and on others in the book of Judges? Is it like what happened to David when Samuel anointed him (1 Samuel 16:13) or to those dry bones Ezekiel saw in the valley (Ezekiel 37) when the breath of the Lord came into them and they came together, bone to bone? Is this how we know what it means that the Spirit drove Jesus—not invited, not suggested, but gave him no choice?

And what is this wilderness? Who has been there before Jesus? Hagar was there, pregnant with Abraham's child, running away from cruel treatment. And Joseph was there, dumped into a pit and then sold by his brothers into slavery. In fact, the Torah—the first five books of scripture—is mostly about what happened to the escaped Hebrew slaves in the wilderness. Later Isaiah would speak of a time when this wilderness would be transformed, would bloom and become a place of flowing streams and strong trees.

And what of the forty? Forty days of rain in the time of Noah. Forty years of struggle and of wandering before crossing the Jordan. Forty years of peace in the days of the judges. Forty years David reigned as king. Forty days Elijah fasted as he walked to the mountain of God. And Jonah finally getting to Nineveh and crying out: "Forty days more and Nineveh will be destroyed!" With all these stories, Jesus could hardly have had twelve or twenty or sixty days in the wilderness. It was forty!

The tempter? Read Job to learn about this character. The wild beasts? Read the Noah stories and especially the covenant God makes with humans and animals in this Sunday's first reading. The angels that come to Jesus? The first time we ever hear about an angel in Genesis is in that wilderness with Hagar the slave (Genesis 16:7). After that, there are many comforting angels. See Psalm 91.

The truth is: The story of Jesus needs the stories that went before. Let this Lent be filled with them. Sit every day with the Bible.

> *God of our ancestors, blessed are you in the scriptures. How sweet are your words to my taste, sweeter than honey to my mouth. (Psalm 119:103)*

MONDAY, MARCH 10, 2003

> *Can mortals be righteous before God . . . those who live in houses of clay, whose foundation is in the dust, who are crushed like a moth? Between morning and evening they are destroyed; they perish forever without any regarding it. . . . They die devoid of wisdom.* JOB 4:17, 19-20, 21

WHO IS SPEAKING HERE? It could be one of the writers of psalms. Or it could be the author of one of the gloomier pages of the Wisdom of Solomon. But this particular passage is spoken by one of those who come to help poor Job see the light. It is Eliphaz. Eliphaz thinks that God never brings suffering to an innocent person because there are no innocent persons in the sight of God. We're all guilty. We all suffer for our sins. So, Job, enough of your proclamations of innocence. Sure, you did a lot of good things. But you're human and now you whine on and on because you're feeling a bit of what many people live with their whole lives. Job, you are no worse a person than anybody else, and in fact you are in most ways a good person. But that's just a human view. It must be from God's view that even you are no more than a moth, say, flying around the light, then crushed. And who notices or cares?

The author of Psalm 103 thought a bit like Eliphaz but had a little more to say:

[God] knows how we were made;
    he remembers that we are dust.
As for mortals, their days are like grass;
    they flourish like a flower of the field;
for the wind passes over it, and it is gone,
    and its place knows it no more.
But the steadfast love of the Lord is from everlasting to
    everlasting. . . .
  –Ps. 103:14-17

Why are we still asking these questions about suffering and about evil? Because no answer yet satisfies? Because no answer makes us let go of the question? Lent comes and we have to be a bit like Ivan in *Brothers Karamazov*: we won't look away when the innocent suffer and we won't be satisfied with pious sayings.

But something new is present in our age: five hundred die in an earthquake in Iran, 3000 perish in the World Trade Center, tens of thousands of children die in Iraq because of political judgments, hundreds die in Bangladesh when a crowded boat sinks, millions in Africa are going to die young of AIDS, and then there are the forty thousand who die every day in our world just because we didn't get the food distributed right. We know so much! And we know so little. And we have our own lives to look after. Maybe the answer of Eliphaz is just fine with us?

> *Remember, O God, that we are dust, our days like the day of grass. How then shall we understand the great and small catastrophes of this world? In these days of Lent, lead us in the way of Jesus who is your compassion among us.*

TUESDAY, MARCH 11, 2003

As for me, I would seek God, and to God I would commit my cause. He does great things and unsearchable, marvelous things without number. He gives rain on the earth and sends waters on the fields; he sets on high those who are lowly, and those who mourn are lifted to safety. JOB 5:8-11

AS IT WAS YESTERDAY, our speaker today is Eliphaz: one of those who comes with some timely advice for poor Job. Job has had the nerve to confront God and ask why. We know we're supposed to be on Job's side, but one has to admit: Eliphaz gets some really great lines in this drama. (Eliphaz speaks the whole of chapters 4 and 5 in the book of Job.)

Where will we later in the Bible hear someone echo the statement "sets on high those who are lowly and those who mourn are lifted to safety"? It sounds a lot like the beatitudes: "Blessed are those who mourn, for they will be comforted. Blessed are the meek, for they will inherit the earth." Later on one can only cheer when Eliphaz declares that God saves the needy from the sword of the mighty "so the poor have hope, and injustice shuts its mouth." Amen! Would that it would happen in our time.

We know we've got a good drama when we are one moment on this side, the next moment won over to the other, then back again. That's Job; and reading and studying Job would be a fine Lenten project.

Eliphaz is also eloquent about the creativity of God: great things and unsearchable, marvelous things without number. Now where will this be echoed? Right in the very book of Job. Eliphaz has given us a preview of what will happen when, after all Job's praying and moaning and clamoring before God, God answers from the whirlwind. And does God have some clincher of an argument? Not at all. Perhaps it isn't about arguments. Perhaps it is about poetry. And God gets the best poetry as God spins out what Eliphaz has said so briefly.

Job has battered God with questions, and what does God say: "Now I will question you, and you shall declare to me"

(38:3). And the questions begin. Pages of them, but all with this general thrust: "Where were you, Job, when I laid the foundation of the earth? Have you commanded the morning? Have the gates of death been revealed to you? Have you comprehended the expanse of the earth? Tell me, Job, the way to the dwelling of light!" And on and on. God answers an angry child the way parents always do: "Don't you know what I have done, and done for you? End of argument." But read it yourself.

> *God of the whirlwind, you fill us with questions. Make us still in this brief Lent to hear around us your own questions for us. And let the cycle continue as we cling to you.*

WEDNESDAY, MARCH 12, 2003

> *"All these I will give you, if you will fall down and worship me." Jesus said to him, "Away with you, Satan! for it is written, 'Worship the Lord your God, and serve only him.'"* MATTHEW 4:9-10

AFTER FORTY DAYS in the wilderness, days with the wild beasts and no human companions, days of discipline, there comes this testing time. The gospel writer puts the whole struggle of all Jesus' life into three face-to-face confrontations. Perhaps it seems to us that the temptations come now because Jesus is at his weakest after such an ordeal. But what we find, and this is what must draw us on into our Lent, is that the ordeal, the fast, has made Jesus strong.

The hardest is the last, the temptation to fall down and worship anything that isn't God. But Jesus, fasting, was himself living by the word of God, nourished by the word of God, chewing over the word of God. So when he comes to this temptation to idolatry, Jesus grasps for and shouts at Satan what must have been for a faithful Jewish person the very core of God's word.

We find it in the book of Deuteronomy, the final book of the Torah, chapters 5 and 6 especially. The story is of Moses convening the whole people—in the wilderness!—and telling them what God has sent him to tell, a covenant. It begins: "I am the LORD your God, who brought you out of the land of Egypt, out of the house of slavery; you shall have no other gods before me" (Deut. 5:6-7).

The other terms of the covenant follow this one, and they are spoken one by one. But then as if to draw it all together, the verses come that include what Jesus will know and speak:

Hear, O Israel: The LORD is our God, the LORD alone. You shall love the LORD your God with all your heart, and with all your soul, and with all your might. Keep these words that I am commanding you today in your heart. Recite them to your children and talk about them when you are at home and when you are away, when you lie down and when you rise. Bind them as a sign on your hand, fix them as an emblem on your forehead, and write them on the door posts of your house and on your gates. The LORD your God you shall fear; him you shall serve. . . .

–Deut. 6:4-9, 13

What an amazing concept here! Keep these words. Recite these words. Talk about these words at home and away, when you rest and when you rise. Put these words on your body and on your house.

One of the tasks of the community in Lent was and is the discernment of idolatry. Where are the other gods? What are their names? How are we worshiping them? How are we to stop?

God of the covenant, of Moses and of Jesus, you alone are our God. Inside and out, let us know and name and turn from any other god, living in your service alone.

THURSDAY, MARCH 13, 2003

Give me neither poverty nor riches; feed me with the food that I need, or I shall be full, and deny you, and say, "Who is the LORD?" or I shall be poor, and steal, and profane the name of my God.
PROVERBS 30:8-9

WISDOM. SOME HAVE PRIZED WISDOM, made it their pursuit. Some of what such people then said has been written down and is there for us in books like Proverbs. Of course, some of this writing was too immediate to make the transition over centuries and cultures. But some of it shows us how constant are our human ways.

The verses above are cast as a prayer to God, the source of wisdom. If we were to put it in other words, we might have: God, I do not want to be rich and I do not want to be poor. If I were rich, if I had more than I need, I would not need you. I would turn away from you and ask, "The Lord? Who is the Lord?" For I would have other lords. But if I were poor, if I did not have even what I need to live, I would steal and do other things that would be wrong.

So far, so good. Most of us aren't that rich, aren't that poor. But the rich are still with us and so are the poor. Most of us grow up with a strong awareness of the rich. Those who have money beyond any need have their faces all over the media. We are supposed to think that what's good for the millionaires and the billionaires will somehow be good for all of us.

Except for an occasional heart-rending story, the poor generally make public appearances only as statistics or criminals. We are told that our economic system needs a fair number of people to be employed at jobs where they will barely get by, and probably stay in debt year after year.

Most of us think we are somewhere, like the writer of the Proverb prays for, in between. But there is this complication: We are part of a huge and intricate economic system, and seen from a global perspective, we are not in the middle at all. We're part of the very, very wealthy of the world.

We have all seen the numbers relating to poverty and wealth, and we've all seen the pictures of poverty's ravages. We probably do what we can to help the poor, especially when some new disaster strikes them. Now comes Lent when our fasting gives us a chance to feel for a moment just one bit of poverty (and none of its hopelessness). But something else is there also in Lent. It has been called almsgiving, but that seems to describe the form it took in other economies. For us, the heart of this Lenten almsgiving is this: What we thought was ours, isn't. In that insight lies wisdom.

O Wisdom, raising our curiosity, teasing our cer-
tainties, playing with possibilities: In this Lent
open our eyes to see that nothing is ours except as
your gift to be given again and again, handed on,
growing.

FRIDAY, MARCH 14, 2003

Always be ready to make your defense to anyone
who demands from you an accounting for the
hope that is in you; yet do it with gentleness and
reverence. 1 PETER 3:15-16

WHEN DOES THAT HAPPEN? Are you stopped in traffic
some day and a stranger knocks on your car window
and, when you crack it open an inch, asks: "What are you
hoping for? And especially, why?" Are we prepared to tell?
And how did the person know we were hoping at all? What
did we do? What did we say? What look was on the face?

Here is something John Wesley wrote in the eighteenth century about a Christian community where there was apparently
not a look of hope on their faces. Then something happened.

A few months ago the generality of people in this circuit
were exceedingly lifeless. Samuel Meggot, perceiving this,
advised the society at Barnard Castle to observe every Friday
with fasting and prayer. The very first Friday they met together, God broke in upon them in a wonderful manner; and
God's work has been increasing among them ever since. The
neighboring societies heard of this, agreed to follow the same
rule, and soon experienced the same blessing. Is not the neglect of this plain duty (I mean fasting, ranked by our Lord
with almsgiving and prayer) one general occasion of dead-
ness among Christians? Can anyone willingly neglect it and
be guiltless?

–The Journal of John Wesley (Moody Press)

Lent is a little like a gymnasium, a fitness center where the
flabby become firm. But fitness centers cater to individuals. Lent
does not. As in Wesley's story, Lent is about the whole church

getting into shape: the fasting, the prayer, the almsgiving—all done knowing we are with each other in these disciplines, in discovering this joyful way. Together we are acquiring habits that cause people to knock on the car windows or the front door and say: "Excuse me, but I have been watching you and I saw what you've been doing with your money. And I saw how you spend your time. And I have heard the tone of your voice and how you speak to all alike. You must be full of hope, despite everything that's going on these days. You must be hoping for something extraordinary because otherwise, it makes no sense!" And, looking back at the verse from 1 Peter, prepare your answer, always with "gentleness and reverence."

Wesley says, "God broke in upon them in a wonderful manner." Can "them" become "us"?

> Break in upon us, O God, as together our household, our congregation, our church strives to keep the ways of Lent. Hold us in your love that we might venture where we have not gone before.

SATURDAY, MARCH 15, 2003

> You keep my eyelids from closing; I am so troubled that I cannot speak. . . . Will the Lord spurn forever, and never again be favorable? . . . Has God forgotten to be gracious? PSALM 77:4, 7, 9

HERE IN PSALM 77 (see all of verses 1 to 15) is the prayer of lamentation. In the days after September 11, 2001, many American Christians seemed to know that this was a language we needed, but it was a language we had forgotten. We could speak of grief and of anger, but lamentation is a prayer that goes beyond these. Lent itself, meeting us each year with hard questions, could be our school for learning this language of lament.

Notice in Psalm 77 that lamentation is not "How could God let such-and-such happen to me?" Lamentation is a language of word and of gesture and of deed. It doesn't try to make everything neat. It doesn't ask God for an explanation, because the one who laments is not willing to accept an explanation. The sorrow is beyond any explaining.

If we look at Psalm 77 we find these verbs and phrases that might offer a glimpse of what it is to lament: I cry aloud, I seek, my hand is stretched out, my soul refuses comfort, I moan, my spirit faints, you keep my eyelids from closing, I cannot speak. Other psalms of lamentation would bring us to other deeds: not eating because appetite is gone, weeping, groaning. We hear also in Psalm 77 that lamentation speaks in bitter questions: Will God spurn forever? Has God's love ceased forever? Are God's promises at an end? Has God forgotten?

Perhaps we think of lamentation as something primitive: the wailing of mourners at a burial. "We don't do that sort of thing." But our scriptures do! They are not afraid of lament, not afraid of its bitter questions, not afraid of its anger. They are not afraid because lamentation is an intimate language within our covenant with God. In fact, God also laments. God also asks bitter questions of us. We can do this because we are bound together in a love that is deep enough, large enough, to allow lamentation. It must allow lamentation.

With Psalm 77, with the Lamentations of Jeremiah, with Psalms 22 and 88 and 137, practice the language of lament during Lent. Jesus, we are told, was speaking and praying one of those psalms on the cross when he cried, "My God, my God, why have you forsaken me?"

> *In the day of my trouble I seek you, Lord. In the night my hand is stretched out without wearying. My soul refuses to be comforted. I think of you and I moan. I meditate, and my spirit faints. (from Psalm 77:2-3)*

SECOND SUNDAY IN LENT, MARCH 16, 2003

> *God said to Abraham, "As for Sarai your wife . . . I will bless her, and moreover I will give you a son by her."* GENESIS 17:15-16

AT THE GREAT VIGIL on the night between Holy Saturday and Easter, they will all be there: Eve, Adam, Noah, Sarah, Abraham, Isaac. All of them and so many more. Every Lent our reading of scripture sends us to ponder again the stories of the ancestors.

We know that what came to be the book of Genesis is a weaving together of various traditions without worrying about smoothing it all out. Sometimes it seems we are getting the same story from two or more angles. It's as if to say: More important than the facts are the stories. The stories are what matter to us, what we take in and ponder and so come to know better our own predicament.

The quote today is from Genesis. In the next verse, right after God has spoken this amazing promise, what happens? Listen. "Then Abraham fell on his face and laughed, and said to himself, 'Can a child be born to a man who is a hundred years old? Can Sarah, who is ninety years old, bear a child?'" (17:17). Abraham, the great model of faithfulness, who left his home in the fertile crescent at God's word, who went through adventure after adventure, this Abraham falls on his face and laughs when God has told him what's to happen? Abraham not only doesn't believe it, he thinks God's lost a grip on the situation. In the next verse, Abraham reminds God: "You already gave me a child. Why don't you come through for Hagar's son Ishmael?" But that's another story.

Then comes Genesis 18, another version of the same promise to Abraham. But in this version the promise comes after Abraham and Sarah offer lavish hospitality to three wanderers. When they respond with a promise about Sarah having a child, Abraham does not fall down laughing. This time it is Sarah who laughs. She laughs at the thought of such an old woman bearing a child, then she denies she laughed. The child to be born will be called "laughter," Isaac, a lifelong (then centuries-long) reminder that both dad and mom just could not believe the news. Where perhaps does a little "Isaac," a little laughter in the presence of God, fit into our Lent?

> *God full of promises, God of our adventurous ancestors, guide this church through the days of Lent, attentive to the scriptures, attentive to the world.*

MONDAY, MARCH 17, 2003

The LORD dealt with Sarah as he had said, and the LORD did for Sarah as he had promised. Sarah conceived and bore Abraham a son in his old age.
GENESIS 21:1-2

CENTURIES AGO THE CHURCH probably gave a winter solstice date to the birth of Jesus because the scripture says that Jesus died at Passover, which is always near the beginning of spring. And, some said, that meant he had to have been conceived at the beginning of spring so the whole cycle would be complete. Some churches still keep March 25 as the feast of the Annunciation and tell the story of the angel's proclamation to Mary and Mary's acceptance. Nine months later it is Christmas.

Stories of wondrous conceptions and births abound in our scriptures. Abraham and Sarah are 100 and 90 years old respectively when Isaac is born a full quarter century after God's first promise—they're so old that both of them laughed at the very idea (see yesterday's reflection). But this is not the first such story. The first story is that of Hagar and her child Ishmael. Genesis 16 says that Hagar is Sarah's "slave girl" and Sarah gives her to Abraham because it seems the only hope of a child. Hagar becomes pregnant and the situation deteriorates and the young woman runs away. But an angel finds her in the wilderness and here is where we find God's promise about a child-to-come: "Now you have conceived and shall bear a son; you shall call him Ishmael, for the LORD has given heed to your affliction" (16:11). (In Genesis 21 there is another story of God's care for Hagar and Ishmael.)

A generation later, "Isaac prayed to the LORD for his wife, because she was barren; and the LORD granted his prayer, and his wife Rebekah conceived" (25:21). And a generation later, after Leah has borne seven children with Jacob, "God remembered Rachel, and God heeded her and opened her womb. . . . and she named [her son] Joseph" (30:22, 24). So it goes. When the people are in hard times with the Philistines, "the angel of the LORD appeared to the woman and said to her, 'Although you are barren . . . you shall conceive and bear a son. . . . It is he who shall begin to deliver Israel from the hand of the Philistines'" (Judges 13:3, 5). This is Samson. And another such birth is that of Samuel. Hannah's prayer and weeping and fasting and promises continued until "the LORD remembered her" (1 Samuel 1:19). Hannah's prayer in 1 Samuel 2 is the song Mary will echo in Luke's telling of the visit to Elizabeth when both of them are pregnant.

So we remember these women, named and unnamed, mighty in their hope and their deeds.

> *We praise you, Lord, for the promises and the births. In this Lenten springtime, let every birth renew in us the wonder at creation. Help us to be bearers of new life for all the world to see.*

TUESDAY, MARCH 18, 2003

[God] said [to Abraham], "Do not lay your hand on the boy or do anything to him." GENESIS 22:12

LENT IS NO RETREAT from hard questions. It is a retreat *into* hard questions, the ones we may be passing by the rest of the year. Lent is death-and-life time. At Easter an old song has it: Life and death have fought, and the champion of life died— and lives now victorious.

In the spring of 2002 the United States Supreme Court ruled that mentally handicapped people could not be executed. This was one more moment in a long national discussion about the death penalty. There are people of goodwill on both sides of the debate, including many who are bothered by the possibility of innocent blood being shed in the pursuit of justice. With the help of DNA testing and through the work of journalists and others, it has been shown that innocent persons have been sentenced to death. How do we deal with that? Then we must confront discrimination: as punishment for the same crimes, non-whites and the poor are far more likely to be executed than whites and the well off. Some who admit these problems still believe they can be fixed and the death penalty retained. Others say the only solution is not to tempt ourselves to put anyone to death.

But even if the death penalty were abolished, hard questions would remain. Like the children in William Golding's novel *Lord of the Flies*, we may escape from terror and death on the island and find ourselves on a warship, out to deal death to some other nation's people. Even if we refrained from administering death within our society, are we any better off if we still administer death to others? What became of that angel that grabbed the hand of Abraham?

In eastern churches the icons of the great Saint Nicholas show many scenes from his life. Often there is one in which an executioner is about to behead several criminals. But Nicholas, fully vested in his bishop clothes, has come up behind the executioner and has reached up to take hold of the man's sword so he cannot bring it down on the criminals. Nicholas was doing what the angel did. Lent should show us where to do our part. And maybe Abraham can be another model for us: think how he almost argued God out of destroying Sodom and Gomorrah (Genesis 18). The only problem was that he stopped at ten.

> *God of all peoples, your child Jesus Isaac-like climbed the mountain carrying the wood of sacrifice. Strengthen us in our Lenten disciplines to live the gospel as proclamation of your love for all the world.*

WEDNESDAY, MARCH 19, 2003

> *[The disciples] were on the road, going up to Jerusalem, and Jesus was walking ahead of them; they were amazed, and those who followed were afraid.* MARK 10:32

MARK'S GOSPEL IN A SINGLE VERSE! Lots of being on the road, determination to get to Jerusalem even though it was becoming clear what would happen there, Jesus out in front of the bumbling disciples ("amazed" is putting a positive spin on their feelings), and fear. The gospel that fills much of this year is that of Mark: no long sermons, no major parables, no infancy or childhood stuff. But there is a lot of action, a lot of conflict with visible and invisible enemies, a lot of wonder working, and—compared to what has gone before—a lot about the passion. And little or nothing about resurrection (depending on how one deals with the various later endings to Mark's gospel). It may be that the original author, the first to write down a gospel that has come down to us, may have been finished when 16:8 was written: "So they went out and fled from the tomb, for terror and amazement had seized them; and they said nothing to anyone, for they were afraid." If so, then the reader of this gospel is left with that amazement and that fear that have been like a refrain through all its pages.

Mark is the gospel of the second year of the three-year cycle of Sunday readings for those churches that use this pattern. Matthew is the first year, Luke the third. The gospel of John isn't read in this way but scattered here and there, especially in Lent (we'll be breaking away from Mark to read from John on the next three Sundays, then on Palm Sunday come back to hear the Passion from Mark), during the holy days of the Triduum, and in the Easter season.

In this three-year cycle, where each year we read week-by-week, in much of the year, through a single evangelist, we get a sense for how the early Christians were telling of Jesus in a variety of ways. In this year of reading Mark, take the verse above as a powerful summary of Mark's Jesus and those around Jesus. Take it as a mantra for the rest of Lent and let it shape how you keep these days. On the road. To Jerusalem. Jesus out in front. Ourselves amazed. And scared.

But scared together. On the road together. What are we getting ourselves into?

> God of our Savior Jesus Christ, when we look around and look ahead, we are justly afraid. Help us to walk with Jesus and with each other, knowing ever more clearly the cost of discipleship.

THURSDAY, MARCH 20, 2003

Your hurt is incurable, your wound is grievous.
There is no one to uphold your cause, no
medicine for your wound, no healing for you. All
your lovers have forgotten you; they care nothing
for you. JEREMIAH 30:12-14

JEREMIAH IS ANOTHER BOOK of the Bible that could well be our daily reading in Lent, along with a good commentary. This reluctant prophet, someone who would rather have just passed his days as another unknown citizen, may be an especially powerful model for those of us who find it all too easy to look away, to keep our mouths closed, to keep ourselves private, to hope that it will be enough to do some quiet good for the world without having to be seen and heard.

Or maybe not! Maybe reading Jeremiah will convince us to keep our heads down and our lips buttoned and let someone else raise the hard questions about justice and fidelity in the world and in the church. After all, who wants to be celibate for life just to make a point about the grim future (ch. 16), or end up at the bottom of a cistern (ch. 38) or on trial for treason (ch. 26) or in prison for desertion (ch. 37)?

This is not an easy book. Jeremiah is full of lamentation. The people also lament as in 14:19 when they ask God: "Have you completely rejected Judah? Does your heart loathe Zion? Why have you struck us down so that there is no healing for us? We look for peace, but find no good; for a time of healing, but there is terror instead." Even God must lament: "I have given the beloved of my heart into the hands of her enemies. My heritage has become to me like a lion in the forest; she has lifted up her voice against me—therefore I hate her" (12:7-8).

Jeremiah's own laments are stronger yet: "Woe is me, my mother, that you ever bore me, a man of strife and contention to the whole land!" (15:10). Why does he go on inviting persecution, derision, isolation? He has pondered this also: "The word of the LORD has become for me a reproach and derision all day long. If I say, 'I will not mention him, or speak any more in his name,' then within me there is something like a burning fire shut up in my bones; I am weary with holding it in" (20:8-9).

"Something like a burning fire shut up in my bones." We began Lent in ashes, and when Lent ends a burning fire begins the great Vigil liturgy. What must we do to get from the ashes to the fire, the fire of Jeremiah, in our congregation, in our very bones?

> O LORD, *you know. Remember me and visit me.*
> *Your words were found, and I ate them, and your*
> *words became to me a joy and the delight of my*
> *heart; for I am called by your name, O* LORD,
> *God of hosts. (from Jeremiah 15:15, 16)*

FRIDAY, MARCH 21, 2003

All of these [Abel, Enoch, Noah, Abraham, Sarah,
their descendents] . . . confessed that they were
strangers and foreigners on the earth, for people
who speak in this way make it clear that they are
seeking a homeland. HEBREWS 11:13-14

WHEN THE AUTHOR OF HEBREWS has finished extolling the ancestors, not only the great names but those whose names have been lost forever, we read this: "Therefore, since we are surrounded by so great a cloud of witnesses, let us also lay aside every weight and the sin that clings so closely, and let us run with perseverance the race that is set before us, looking to Jesus the pioneer and perfecter of our faith" (12:1-2).

Run the race that is set before us! So we are. That is what we are making of Lent, not the race itself but the training for the race. Getting the body and heart and mind and spirit in shape for the race. Laying aside the sin that clings so closely. That is not easily done, of course. If it were, what need would we have for Lent? And it is not something one person does alone. Most of it has to be done in the household and by the congregation, all straining together so that each of us has this "cloud of witnesses" not only as the ones who have gone ahead but those people right there with me on Sunday. We are all of us the strangers and the foreigners on the earth, aren't we? We're the ones seeking a homeland, right? Isn't that the point of the race we're training for, to get there together?

In Hebrews 11 the refrain is "by faith." It is said that "by faith" Noah built an ark (v. 7), "by faith Rahab the prostitute did not perish with those who were disobedient" (v. 31). We may waver a bit when we get to those who "by faith" were stoned to death, sawn in two, went about in skins of sheep and goats, wandered in deserts and mountains. That's not all. In the midst of Lent, we could take time to add to Hebrews 11. We have known—personally or at a distance—some who have lived by faith. We might write sentences that begin, "By faith, Aunt Harriet . . ." "By faith, Dietrich Bonhoeffer . . ." "By faith!"

> *Jesus, pioneer of our faith, who endured the cross for the sake of the joy that was set before you, we look to you in these Lenten days and with you give thanks to the Father that we are surrounded by so great a cloud of witnesses.*

SATURDAY, MARCH 22, 2003

> *O give thanks to the LORD, call on his name, make known his deeds among the peoples. Sing to him, sing praises to him; tell of all his wonderful works.* PSALM 105:1-2

THOSE ARE TWO THINGS that Jews and Christians practice and practice and practice. Giving thanks, telling the wonderful works. This Psalm 105 is about to launch into such an exercise in giving thanks and telling the wonders (not unlike what happened in Hebrews 11, read yesterday). The verb that has to go with the thanking and the telling is one we use all the time: Remember. Psalm 105:5 says, "Remember the wonderful works [God] has done, his miracles, and the judgments he has uttered."

Lent, this time of getting into our Christian shape, is for asking: How skilled are we at giving thanks and at telling the wonderful works? That is not a matter of eloquence, but a matter of habit. Are we in the habit of giving God thanks? That is the core prayer of our assembly, sometimes called eucharist: giving thanks. But the prayer we do at the table of the assembly on Sunday both echoes and inspires the daily habit of thanksgiving. That is our way to be in this world. Don't get it confused with rose-colored glasses! Rather, the habit of giving thanks is the very ground we walk on, the foundation we build on. We look straight-on at the hardship and the evil *because* we are people founded in thanksgiving. Otherwise, how could we? We tell the wonderful works of God because we know well all the not-so-wonderful stuff that goes on with me, with my house, with my nation, with my earth. The awful stuff could overwhelm us if we didn't know how to give thanks and tell the wonderful works of God—in and for the same world! We shall overcome because we give thanks, because we tell.

This is in our baptized bones. We rehearse it in the Sunday assembly, in morning prayer and night prayer, at table. We are people who remember, who turn the story over and over and so recognize that it isn't going to be a story about long ago and far away, but always a tale about God and this church—me, the household, the congregation. Psalm 105:8 proclaims: "[God] is mindful of his covenant . . . for a thousand generations." Count them. Make sure God remembers. Make sure we remember.

Rehearse our lips and our hearts, blessed God, in the ways of giving thanks to you at every time and in every place, despite everything, because of everything. In what we say and what we do these days of Lent may your wonderful works be known.

THIRD SUNDAY IN LENT, MARCH 23, 2003

Has not God made foolish the wisdom of the world? For since, in the wisdom of God, the world did not know God through wisdom, God decided, through the foolishness of our proclamation, to save those who believe. . . . We proclaim Christ crucified. 1 CORINTHIANS 1:20-21, 23

THIS READING FROM 1 Corinthians comes in the midst of other Sunday readings today: the commandments given to Moses in Exodus and the story in John's gospel of how Jesus, early in his ministry, went to the temple and set it free of all that was not at home there. If there's a thread, it's tension. The commandment-giving happens on the mountain "on the morning of the third day"(Ex. 19:16) and there is cloud and thunder and lightning and earthquake and a great deal of consternation among the terrified people. In the gospel, the people going about their business as usual in the temple are suddenly confronted by this zealot who never bothered to ask them first whether they had permission to be there, never bothered even to warn them that if they didn't leave, there'd be trouble.

And Paul is starting his letter to the church at Corinth—where he'd heard there was all sorts of unpleasantness going on—with this mighty proclamation: If you wanted miracles and power, you came to the wrong meeting. If you wanted to ponder the thoughts of great gurus, wrong meeting. What we have here, Paul reminds the church, is neither power nor wisdom, but weakness and foolishness. What can you expect from a Jesus who turned down the stone-into-bread temptation and the all-the-kingdoms-of-the-world temptation? The only power we have, Paul says, the only wisdom we have is this: the cross. He goes on to say it isn't just about Jesus: "God chose what is low and despised in the world, things that are not, to reduce to nothing things that are" (1:28).

As we muddle through Lent, we turn more and more toward the cross, preparing to acclaim it on Good Friday when all that weakness and foolishness of God is told and pondered and venerated. The church has long sung it this way:

Bend your boughs, O Tree of glory!
All your rigid branches, bend!
For a while the ancient temper
That your birth bestowed, suspend;
And the king of earth and heaven
Gently on your bosom tend.

–*Pange lingua*, tr. J.M. Neale, alt.

The church sings to the cross as to a mother or a grandmother, as to one who will throw off the assigned role of pain and torture and instead cuddle this Christ on her bosom.

*Take this church of yours further into Lent, dear
God, where we may find in our own days and our
own community the weakness and the foolishness
of the cross.*

MONDAY, MARCH 24, 2003

*Then the officials said to the king, "This man
ought to be put to death, because he is discourag-
ing the soldiers who are left in this city, and all the
people, by speaking such words to them. For this
man is not seeking the welfare of this people, but
their harm." King Zedekiah said, "Here he is; he
is in your hands."* JEREMIAH 38:4-5

TWENTY-THREE YEARS AGO TODAY in the city of San Salvador the archbishop was shot to death as he presided at
the celebration of the eucharist. This was Oscar Romero. He
had been a quiet intellectual, rather conservative, a better
friend to the elites than to the masses, when he became the
archbishop just a few years before his death. But very quickly
he became the voice of those who were being oppressed in El
Salvador. When the military and the paramilitary murdered
priests who worked with the poor, when the poor themselves
were tortured and murdered, when outside interests—including the government of the United States—gave money and
weapons and encouragement to the deeds of those in control
of the country, here was Romero speaking out. On the
church's radio station his words were carried to all. Like
Jeremiah, he spoke the word no matter the consequences.

What is the source of such courage? Two days before he
died, Romero spoke in his Sunday preaching directly to the
military: Stop the killing, he told them. I order you to stop.
And he took his place with the thousands of twentieth-century
martyrs in the Christian tradition, witnesses to Christ, those
who refused to let the church be a bystander when evil was
being done. Here is how Romero spoke of this: "The church
takes as spittle in its face, as lashes on its back, as the cross in

its passion, all that human beings suffer, even though they be unbelievers" (Sermon, Dec. 31, 1977).

And these words also, perhaps for us: "To each one of us Christ is saying: 'If you want your life and mission to be fruitful like mine, do as I. Be converted into a seed that lets itself be buried. Let yourself be killed. Do not be afraid. Those who shun suffering will remain alone. No one is more alone than the selfish. But if you give your life out of love for others, as I give mine for all, you will reap a great harvest'" (Sermon, Apr. 1, 1979).

> *God of martyrs, for your poor ones you raise up voices that cry out as did Archbishop Romero. Give us courage to risk what we must if the lives of the poor are to be saved.*

TUESDAY, MARCH 25, 2003

> *Do not be afraid, Mary, for you have found favor with God. And now, you will conceive in your womb and bear a son, and you will name him Jesus.* LUKE 1:30-31

OSCAR ROMERO PUT ON Christ's lips, in the text quoted at the end of yesterday's reflection, an exhortation to us. It includes the words the angel speaks in Luke's gospel to Mary: "Do not be afraid." In fact, these must be words we all need to hear for they appear again and again in our scriptures. God tells Abram, "Do not be afraid." God tells Isaac this. The midwife tells Rachel this as she is in labor with Benjamin. Joseph tells his terrified brothers in Egypt: Do not be afraid. So it goes through the stories. In the gospels, Luke's angel speaks these words first to Zechariah, then to Mary, then to the shepherds. Matthew's angel has Joseph hear them in a dream. Jesus walking on the sea tells the trembling disciples, "Do not be afraid." And he tells Peter, James, and John the same thing after the transfiguration. In Matthew's telling of the risen Jesus, there are again angels to say to the women, "Do not be afraid," and then Jesus himself tells them.

All of these people, our ancestors, had reasons to be afraid. This is not simply the stuff of living a normal life with all the fear that brings—for the family, for the future, for safety, for health. They are also afraid because of the situations they are in, because of the tasks they have to carry out. But fear is also what happens to us when we are in the presence of God, of God's messenger. In all, it seems we are to get ourselves into fearful predicaments as we pursue doing some good on this earth, knowing we'll always have in our ears this mantra: "Do not be afraid."

The poet William Butler Yeats wrote of the annunciation (which the church observes today) and of Mary's fear, not just then but ever after. His poem ends with Mary speaking:

What is this flesh I purchased with my pains,
This fallen star my milk sustains,
This love that makes my heart's blood stop
Or strikes a sudden chill into my bones
And bids my hair stand up?

–"The Mother of God," in *The Collected Poems of W.B. Yeats* (Simon
& Schuster)

Can we expect any less if we take this gospel to heart? It is our Lenten work to live so that the "heart's blood stop" and the "chill into my bones" and the "hair stand up" are ours too.

> *Lord, fill our hearts with your grace: once, through the message of an angel you revealed to us the incarnation of your Son; now, through his suffering and death lead us to the glory of his resurrection. (Angelus prayer)*

WEDNESDAY, MARCH 26, 2003

> *Wherever I have moved about among all the people of Israel, did I ever speak a word with any of the tribal leaders of Israel, . . . saying, "Why have you not built me a house?"* 2 SAMUEL 7:7

THIS IS WHAT THE LORD says to Nathan at night just a few hours after David told Nathan that he had in mind to build a house for the Lord. Why should he, David, have a house and the Lord not? Nathan agreed, but God had the above and more to say. Nathan listened to God. David listened to Nathan. It would be Solomon who would next try to build a house for God, but only with disclaimers (1 Kings 8:27).

Today and the next few days, sparked by last Sunday's gospel story of Jesus' deeds in the temple when he saw all the commerce going on there, we reflect on what we are doing when we build and use churches. It's pretty clear we aren't making a house for God. What then?

We are making a space where we can do those deeds that we have made our own from the tradition—deeds of assembling, welcoming, listening to the word of God and pondering and preaching, interceding, giving thanks, baptizing, marrying, burying, keeping vigil, sharing the holy communion. We need a room to do all those deeds. It's all about verbs. We gather to do things, even still and silent things. But we do most of this with singing, which makes its own demands on the room. And we do it with all the beauty in image and speech and gesture that we can summon. We do it with a certain fullness that means abundant water for baptizing and fragrant oil for anointing and real bread and wine for the table.

One document puts it this way: "Christians have not hesitated to use every human art in their celebration of the saving work of God in Jesus Christ, although in every historical period they have been influenced, at times inhibited, by cultural circumstances. In the resurrection of the Lord, all things are made new. Wholeness and healthiness are restored, because the reign of sin and death is conquered. Human limits are still real and we must be conscious of them. But we must also praise God and give God thanks with the human means we have available. God does not need liturgy; people do, and people have only their own arts and styles of expression with which to celebrate" (*Environment and Art in Catholic Worship*, #4).

"Praise God and give God thanks with the human means," it says. And: "God does not need liturgy, people do." Are the halls where we gather up to these expectations? Open enough, honest enough, and somehow beautiful?

It is all yours, O God. The heavens and the high-
est heavens cannot contain you, much less the
houses we build. But hear the plea of your people
when they pray. Hear and heed and forgive.
(Based on 1 Kings 8:27-30)

THURSDAY, MARCH 27, 2003

My house shall be called a house of prayer for all
the nations. MARK 11:17

WHEN A BUILDING IS BEING DEDICATED by Roman Catholics as a place of the church's liturgy and prayer, the rite includes this prayer:

Here may the waters of baptism overwhelm the shame of
sin; here may your people die to sin and live again
through grace as your children.

Here may your children, gathered around your altar, celebrate the memorial of the Paschal Lamb, and be fed at
the table of Christ's word and Christ's body.

Here may prayer, the church's banquet, resound through
heaven and earth as a plea for the world's salvation.

Here may the poor find justice, the victims of oppression,
true freedom.

From here may the whole world, clothed in the dignity of the
children of God, enter with gladness your city of peace.

–Rite of Dedication of a Church, #62.

Ponder the verbs and other action words: overwhelm, die,
live, gather, celebrate, be fed, resound, find (Is this hardest but
most important of all? Notice who is to do the finding and
what they/we are to find), clothed, enter. It isn't a complete list
of what is to go on in the worship center, but it is a good start.

Those are the deeds we need to do and, when possible, we
find or we build a proper space to do them in. Little by little, the
doing of these deeds forms us to be gospel people first and last,
gets the gospel-living into how we think and act and do our
daily life. The deeds done in the space are a kind of training in
holiness, a training to recognize the Holy One in every epiphany

day by day, a training in how to do this world's life that will send the money-changers running—or turn them around. And if such spaces can do their work and do it better by showing forth the painting and sculpture—the fabric and vessels that themselves are worthy art and so for us icons of an incarnate God—then let it be. The good work of human arts should be at home with us more than anywhere else.

> Unless you build the house, dear Lord, all of us
> who build it labor in vain. Be with us day by day
> as we labor to make your whole house, your
> whole earth, a house of prayer for all people.

FRIDAY, MARCH 28, 2003

> Do you not know that you are God's temple and
> that God's Spirit dwells in you? . . . God's temple
> is holy, and you are that temple.
> 1 CORINTHIANS 3:16-17

WITHOUT A MOMENT'S HESITATION, we think that *you,* above, is singular. Me. You too, of course, and that other person over there. Each of us.

But *you* isn't singular. Paul has said that he is like a master builder who has laid a foundation that others can build on (some well, some not). He has said that he is not the foundation of the building. The only foundation is Jesus Christ. So let the building that's to be done be worthy of that foundation! But when he comes to say that this is the Spirit-filled temple we're building, Paul is clear he means the lot of us. This whole assembly is this temple whose foundation is Jesus Christ. This goes beyond saying pretty things about cooperation and hospitality and churchly bonds to one another. What's being built isn't a life here and a life there, lots of individuals with occasional corporate gatherings. No, the only thing being built at all is what we are together. The church.

That makes an immense difference to how we think about ourselves, our deeds, our mission. And such a sense of our corporateness is not easy to have in a society that goes all out to make us so many individuals. ("Bowling alone" is the metaphor with which one author captured our times.) Even in this Lent, we are likely to be looking at how I am doing, and not at all at how this local church is doing. I may fast a few days a week, but when does the church come together to break the common fast with a simple meal of bread and soup? I may be giving alms of my money or time, but when can we share the ways we have found to do this and so build one another and the common spirit? And when we gather on Sundays and the scriptures are proclaimed, how do we go from thinking about "what does this mean to me?" to "how is this church to receive and ponder and take in this word?" When the bread and wine are placed on the table, is it clear that the whole assembled church is giving God thanks and praise?

But if there is to be this building, the *you* is going to be the whole room full of us.

> *In these days of Lent, builder God, weave and forge and pound and hew and cobble together this church we mean to be, little by little giving us the shape of your own Spirit.*

SATURDAY, MARCH 29, 2003

> *My soul longs, indeed it faints for the courts of the LORD; my heart and my flesh sing for joy to the living God.* PSALM 84:2

IT HELPS TO THINK "procession." "I was glad when they said to me: 'Let us go to the house of the Lord'" (Ps. 122:1). We can think of that procession starting with Eve and Adam, joined in by Sarah and Abraham, then into Egypt and back out dryshod through the sea, and later including ordinary people like Peter or Mary Magdalene taking off for far lands. The procession gathers and it fades, it splits and it comes back together. Scriptures are being carried to be read along the way and there is much singing. Sometimes people fast, sometimes they feast. The procession stretches across many borders and many centuries. It is bound for being at home with God. No English writer saw this procession better than Flannery O'Connor. Near the end of her 1964 short story "Revelation" a woman who has known some suffering comes that day at sunset to feed the hogs. She watches them awhile, then looks up and seems to have a vision:

She saw the streak as a vast swinging bridge extending upward from the earth through a field of living fire. Upon it a vast horde of souls were rumbling toward heaven. There were whole companies of white-trash, clean for the first time in their lives, and bands of black niggers in white robes, and battalions of freaks and lunatics shouting and clapping and leaping like frogs. And bringing up the end of the procession was a tribe of people whom she recognized at once as those who, like herself and Claud, had always had a little of everything and the God-given wit to use it right . . . Yet she could see by their shocked and altered faces that even their virtues were being burned away.

–*The Complete Stories* (Farrar, Straus & Giroux)

The woman then returns toward the house, still hearing "the voices of the souls climbing upward into the starry field and shouting hallelujah."

Happily, Lent is not about who gets to be in the procession. Lent is our little group doing the procession. Look around. Be amazed. Be humbled. And get moving!

> *God, ever on the move yet our dwelling place, give us eyes to see all who walk with us here, ears to hear all their shouts and songs, voices in acclaim also. Be our journey and our rest.*

FOURTH SUNDAY IN LENT, MARCH 30, 2003

> *Just as Moses lifted up the serpent in the wilderness, so must the Son-of-Man be lifted up, that whoever believes in him may have eternal life. For God loved the world in this way, that God gave the Son, the only begotten one, so that everyone who believes in him may not perish but may have eternal life.* JOHN 3:14-16 (IN *Readings for the Assembly,* YEAR B, P. 81)

FOR A WHILE, SIGNS SAYING "John 3:16" were showing up with some frequency at sporting events and other places where they might be seen by large numbers of people. John 3:16 is the second sentence in the scripture text above. This desire to get people to go home and look up John 3:16 must be motivated by something strong (other than getting one's face on television). Is it just the sheer literary power of this sentence?

It would be unfortunate if having John 3:16 shoved once too often in our faces meant that we didn't ponder this amazing sentence. But we ponder it in the light of the previous verses and of the whole gospel of John. "Lifted up" is the way the Jesus of John's gospel speaks of the crucifixion, but the very words *lifted up* give new insight. Moses lifted up the serpent and all who looked on it were healed. Jesus must be lifted up. The image is one of triumph, exultation: carrying the victor through the streets. That is exactly right for John, because here the death of Jesus is not one thing and the resurrection another. It is a single mystery, a single act. The lifting up is the saving death that embraces all in life.

Why? Why should such a thing happen? Why should God, Abraham-like, give God's own child, Jesus? That is what John 3:16 is answering. And it is an amazing answer: "For God loved the world." How's that again? Didn't God love Israel? Love the church? Love the righteous? Love sinners? But here it says (and this verse is seen as the summary of John's whole gospel) that God loved the world. And the world is something else for John. The world is that which did not know Jesus (1:10). The world is all that stands against Jesus (15:18). The world is clearly the enemy, to be conquered (16:33). But God so loved the world!

The question is: Do we? Do we love the world as God loves the world? This is a fierce, eyes-wide-open love that's likely to edge into every choice we make.

> God, still loving the world, we look on Jesus who
> is lifted up in the triumph of the cross. Take us
> day by day through this Lent, seeking to be in the
> world as a lover would be.

MONDAY, MARCH 31, 2003

They could not drink the water of Marah because it was bitter. And the people complained against Moses, saying, "What shall we drink?" He cried out to the Lord. EXODUS 15:23-25

A FEW SENTENCES IN EXODUS 15 take us from Miriam's triumphant deliverance song ("Horse and rider [God] has thrown into the sea"[v. 1]) to barely three days later when the people have gone into the wilderness. There's now no water fit to drink. There is bitter water, though, and there are certainly tears from thirsty children and from Moses himself in his cry to the Lord. It didn't take long for the great adventure, the great escape, to turn as bitter as the water of Marah. This is the first of many stories of the grumbling assembly, the go-between deeds of Moses, and the temporary resolution.

In this episode, the "Lord who heals you" brings the congregation to a place called Elim where there are 12 springs of water and 70 palm trees. Even the numbers were handed down in the story. Such springs from God's goodness point to our own Lenten work. A fifth-century preacher can help. Peter Chrysologus talks about the "springs" of mercy:

Mercy is to fasting as rain is to the earth. However much you may cultivate your heart, clear the soil of your nature, root out your vices and sow virtues, if you do not release the springs of mercy, your fasting will not bear fruit. When you fast, what you pour out in mercy overflows into your barn. So do not lose by saving, but gather in by scattering
–*A Word in Season* (Augustinian Press)

"Release the springs of mercy." That is Lent's work. The Lenten fasting (of various kinds: food, wastefulness, entertainment) prepares the ground (note all the elements of Peter's metaphor), but only those springs of mercy are going to bring forth a harvest. And what are they? The various ways of almsgiving, of reordering wealth and power on earth.

Is all this heavy and burdensome? Not if you believe another preacher of the same time, Pope Leo the Great:

Let works of mercy be our delight and let us be filled with those kinds of food that feed us for eternity. Let us rejoice in the replenishment of the poor. . . . Let our humaneness be felt by the sick in their illnesses, by the weakly in their infirmities, by the exiles in their hardships, by the orphans in their destitution, and by solitary widows in their sadness.

–Sermon XL: On Lent

The challenge of a Lent in 2003 is to see the need both in our town and in the wide world, and to work for better ways. That too is almsgiving.

> *With you, Lord who heals, let us open the springs of mercy in our hearts and in our congregation. May our Lenten fast pour out in mercy for those near and far away. May it open our eyes to see what must be done to change the workings of the world.*

TUESDAY, APRIL 1, 2003

> *"Listen, you rebels, shall we bring water for you out of this rock?" Then Moses lifted up his hand and struck the rock twice with his staff; water came out abundantly, and the congregation and their livestock drank.* NUMBERS 20:10-11

YOU REBELS! The story comes alive in words like that. Even infrequently visited books like Numbers come alive! "Why," the people had asked Moses, "why have you brought us up out of Egypt, to bring us to this wretched place? It is no place for grain, or figs, or vines, or pomegranates; and there is no water to drink." This wretched place! And the irony in remembering the good things of Egypt—grain and fruit—while forgetting why they had wanted to leave, and here, they say, here there is no water!

Lent often uses the Exodus story. Lent perhaps *is* the Exodus story. In the wilderness, we can get at each other. We can get angry and shout. Fasting from food does all sorts of good things. One of them ought to be to make us angry. We choose this fast, we choose to be hungry, to know what hunger feels like. But we have an endpoint. It will be over. (And, we know, it can be over any time we choose. It is in our hands.) But not so for thousands and millions in the world. And if our fasting has made us a little closer to them, made us know just some tiny bit of what such a life is like, then we ought to do the rebels' work and cry out: "This wretched place! Why are we in this place? How is it we have a world where people go hungry?" These are not charity questions, they are justice questions. They are questions about a system that gives lip service to ending hunger and poverty, but won't take the steps needed to do it. The questions are Lenten questions because they get at the gospel living we're after. And they are angry questions.

Hunger, of course, is only a part of it. What if we were to fast from all acts of power over others? To somehow identify with the powerless? Or even to identify, in the course of a few days, how often we take to ourselves as for granted what the powers of the world keep from the majority poor, those near and those far away?

> God of the rebels, God of the amazing rock that gives us all water to drink: Take us through these Lenten days in solidarity with the world's poor, willing to raise not only alms but voices on their behalf.

WEDNESDAY, APRIL 2, 2003

> Have you commanded the morning since your days began, and caused the dawn to know its place? Where is the way to the dwelling of light, and where is the place of darkness, that you may take it to its territory and that you may discern the paths to its home? JOB 38:12, 19-20

GOD, INSTEAD OF GIVING JOB a patient answer to the poor man's complaints, seems to be roaring with laughter. "Where were you, Job?" And, "Now tell me, Job." The stanzas of poetry roll on, one wonder after another. Get a grip, Job. It takes nothing away from your questions if God points out that your suffering isn't the whole of creation's story. It doesn't mean you are being ignored if you are told to hold on, look around, and even in your suffering lift up a few words of wonder and give thanks.

Among the marvels God describes for Job are these lovely questions about light. Light, like water in the texts of the last few days, comes more and more frequently into the reading and prayer of the church as Lent moves toward its end, toward the Three Days of the paschal mystery. The center of the year is not a day but a night, the night between Holy Saturday and Easter. The darkness is not a dramatic effect, it is essential to our vigil that begins with a fire and then follows with the candle that will be light for the long time of reading from the scriptures, preparing ourselves to approach the font. One of the earliest songs from that night plays with the notions of light and darkness:

O night more light than day,
    more bright than the sun,
O night more white than snow,
    more brilliant than many torches,
O night of more delight than is paradise.
Night devoid of all dark,
O night dispelling sleep
    and teaching us the vigilance of angels.
O night the demons tremble at,
    night of all nights in all the year desired.
Night of the church's bridal,
    night of new birth in baptism,
    night when the Devil slept and was stripped,
    night when the heir took the heiress
    to enjoy their inheritance.

–Asterius of Amasia, fourth century. *Early Christian Prayers,* ed. A. Hamman, trans. by Walter Mitchell, English translation © 1961 Longmans, Green and Co. Ltd.

Questions arise. Had the author been fasting too long? How can night be "devoid of all dark" and "more bright than the sun"? What wedding is this, while the demons are trembling, and while Satan is being robbed? Robbed of what? And what about the "heir" and "heiress"? What is going on tonight? Have we received our invitations?

Questioning God of the whirlwind, shout at us such questions as to make our eyes open and our ears listen and all our being, however grievous the times, know that you do wonders and will not forget the cries of the poor.

THURSDAY, APRIL 3, 2003

Your sun shall no more go down, or your moon withdraw itself; for the LORD will be your ever-lasting light, and your days of mourning shall be ended. ISAIAH 60:20

A GREAT PART OF KEEPING LENT is letting the images loose, where they can have a real effect on us. We don't try to keep our "real lives" going on one level while on another we take a bit of time for the customs, scriptures, songs, and disciplines of the Forty Days. It all has to hang together. Even the worlds we would otherwise not be paying attention to—the world where deals are made, the earth divided up, the wealthy kept wealthy and the poor made poorer. Lent insists: Open your eyes! Look! This isn't time-out to play church. This is time-in.

Fasting from food and TV and such serves to get clarity about self and world. Part of the reason we fast is to feel the pinch, and part of it is to realize what we can do without from now on, taking a little less of the world that's already so un-equally distributed. We may find that our way of living changes, and we carry Lent's discoveries far beyond Easter.

That is why the giving of alms—of money, goods, time, and talent—isn't limited to a cleaning out of what we don't use anyway. Alms is ultimately about setting things right. That's why fasting and almsgiving is so vital for the Christians of the First World who are part of a society that uses ten or more times its share of the world's resources and, in doing so, does ten times the polluting it should be doing. How will the alms we give go beyond the charity that the well-off can easily af-ford (and take tax deductions for)?

Lent is about individuals being made over, about the household and the congregation being made over—but ultimately it is about the world being made over. "Your days of mourning shall be ended," Isaiah says. For this to happen, for the days of mourning to be ended, they have to have begun and gone on. Something is amiss otherwise. In this age and land, we can easily live on the surface, our minds and selves becoming as shallow and swiftly changed as the images on the TV news: disaster in Brazil, global warming worse, World Court rejected, and now this: new cars! new deodorant! and on to do the stocks, sports, and weather.

But where is the mourning? Only from the mourning that takes us to the depths of our world, our times, comes that light.

> *Lord, you are our everlasting light, sun and moon*
> *and stars for us. In these Lenten days may we see*
> *this world of ours by your light, how delightful*
> *and how sad it is. Help us with the hard question-*
> *ing about what is to be done.*

FRIDAY, APRIL 4, 2003

Esther said in reply to Mordecai, "Go, gather all the Jews to be found in Susa, and hold a fast on my behalf, and neither eat nor drink for three days, night or day. I and my maids will also fast as you do. After that I will go to the king, though it is against the law; and if I perish, I perish."
ESTHER 4:15-16

THERE ARE MANY MOTIVES for fasting. There is a penitential fasting. Scripture tells of what happened when Jonah finally got to Nineveh and began to preach repentance. A fast was proclaimed: "No human being or animal . . . shall taste anything. They shall not feed, nor shall they drink water. Human beings and animals shall be covered with sackcloth, and they shall cry mightily to God. All shall turn from their evil ways and from the violence that is in their hands. Who knows? God may relent" (Jonah 3:7-9). You have to love a proclamation that includes the animals, and that says, "Who knows?"

Then there is the fast of David when the baby born to Bathsheba is ill: "David therefore pleaded with God for the child; David fasted, and went in and lay all night on the ground. On the seventh day the child died" (2 Samuel 12:16, 18). Penitential? Yes, for David confessed his sin. But David also fasts, as do the people of Nineveh, because—Who knows?—God may relent and spare the child.

Then there is the fast of Elijah: forty days on the way to the mountain, escaping with his life. His was not a fast of repenting but of anticipating, of excitement, of being so filled with what is to come. Yet other fasting is about obtaining clarity and discipline and strength; Jesus' fast is like this.

What then of Esther and the Jews when they stand on the brink of annihilation in Persia, desperate to deflect the scheme of Haman? Esther herself is not threatened because neither Haman nor the king knows she is a Jew. But for her people she will risk her life, breaking the law to speak to the king, to expose Haman's plot and plead for the lives of the Jews. She knows how to prepare, whether it is for death or for making the plea. She fasts, but not alone. She calls on the whole community to be in solidarity with her and she is with them.

All of this is our heritage for the gift of Lenten fasting.

> *God of David, of Esther, of Elijah, and of us all: In this season of Lent may we embrace with joy the ways of fasting. In our various hungers, may we grow to cherish all that is good in your creation.*

SATURDAY, APRIL 5, 2003

Their hearts were bowed down with hard labor; they fell down, with no one to help.
PSALM 107:12

OF WHOM DO WE THINK when we hear this psalm verse? Here's one possible group: children of Ecuador who work long days picking and processing the bananas we love to put on our breakfast cereal or under our ice cream or into our smoothie. We have to get that potassium! But the banana comes from somewhere far away. It comes, as do so many things we eat and use, from lands that have been turned into vast plantations for export. This has been the way in much of the world: small farms gone, forests and pastures gone, so that the favorite foods and drinks of the world's few wealthy can be grown—and sold to them cheap enough to compete with the next country.

Here's another possible subject of this single verse: workers in what are rightly called sweatshops. They are Latin American and Asian people who have no health care, bad working conditions, low pay, long hours. In recent years many in the First World have tried to help by boycotts and pressure on the shoe and clothing giants. Sometimes there has been progress. More is needed.

Another possibility. Closer to home, immigrant households with several minimum wage earners, still not rising out of poverty, doing the hardest and most repulsive jobs in the society.

"They fell down, with no one to help." How will we answer for these brothers and sisters? Stockholder pressure, selective buying, letters to Congress and corporations, all have some good to do. But Lent demands getting tough, demands conversion. People are sentenced, beginning often at age six, to lives of hard labor. They fall down. They never have even a shadow of what we somehow take as a right. But it works for somebody—the consumer. And most of us are willing to let it work that way though it makes the world a foul place.

When we dip into the book of Psalms, we should be amazed at what stands side by side there. Some of these psalms cheer on the powers that be. Some carry on against the enemy. But some, like Psalm 107, which is really a psalm of thanksgiving from all those who have been in hard times and come through, are thoroughly subversive. It wasn't the mother of Jesus (Luke 1:46-55) who invented the language of God knocking aside the rich and the powerful and putting the lowly in charge and food on all tables. She seems only to have known and taken to heart Psalm 107 and much else in the tradition.

We thank you, Lord, for your steadfast love, your wonderful works to humankind. You satisfy the thirsty, fill the hungry with good things, shatter the doors of bronze. All this you ask of us as well.

FIFTH SUNDAY IN LENT, APRIL 6, 2003

In the days of his flesh, Jesus offered up prayers and supplications, with loud cries and tears, to the one who was able to save him from death, and he was heard because of his reverent submission.
HEBREWS 5:7

THE SCRIPTURES OF THIS SUNDAY sound like the end of Lent is close. Jeremiah, in a rare moment, forgets gloom and writes of how God is making the covenant anew, writing it on the heart and not on a scroll. And in John 12:24, the words of Jesus tell the paschal mystery: Unless the grain of wheat falls into the ground and dies . . .

But there is also this text from Hebrews 5:7 that is sometimes read again on Good Friday before the account of Jesus' passion and death. These words of "loud cries and tears to the one who was able to save him from death" always come as a shock.

Lent's fasting and Lent's almsgiving go with Lent's prayer. How has that been? With Jesus, are we offering prayers and supplications, perhaps at times with loud cries and tears? What do we know of these loud cries and tears of Jesus? We think of Gethsemane and of how "he threw himself on the ground and prayed" (Matt. 26:39). We think of Jesus' tears: looking at Jerusalem as a mother looks at her children, or approaching the tomb of his friend Lazarus where the gospel text says twice "he was deeply moved" and then "he began to weep." We think too of Luke's stark version of the beatitudes (6:20-21): "Blessed are you who weep now, for you will laugh." We think of the crucified Jesus praying Psalm 22 and this must be loud cries and tears: "My God, my God, why have you forsaken me?"

Lent is not to be a time of year set aside for us to pray. Lent is a school of praying, a time of getting the rhythms of prayer into our lives again so they can stay there all year, all our lives. We learn two things from Jesus' prayer: It was such a habit for him, there by morning and by night (that's one point) that when he saw what was to be seen (that's the second point), he had the words to pray, and the tears, and the gestures. So first: make a habit of prayer, of the psalms and other texts made our own day by day. Second: keep our eyes open to the world so that we can voice every suffering and need and thanksgiving to God.

Let the rhythms of our world and of our lives bring forth prayer to you, God. Open our lips to proclaim your praise and to bring before you again and again the troubles and thanksgivings of the world.

MONDAY, APRIL 7, 2003

Then Susanna cried out with a loud voice, and said, "O eternal God, you know what is secret and are aware of all things before they come to be; you know that these men have given false evidence against me. And now I am to die, though I have done none of the wicked things that they have charged against me!" SUSANNA 42-43 (THE GREEK VERSION OF DANIEL 13:42-43)

FOR CENTURIES THE STORY of Susanna was a weekday reading during Lent. The whole story is found in some ancient texts of the book of Daniel; it is one of those parts of scripture that the churches of the Reformation have placed in the Apocrypha. In any case, it is a story well told, long remembered, and worth exploring—even for Protestants! (The story is only one chapter long.) In outline, the tale is about a beautiful married woman whom two judges try unsuccessfully to seduce. Upon her refusal, they attempt by lying to have her executed, only to have their evil exposed by Daniel. Like most such stories, it is really about many things. Here we have lust and purity, the abuse of power, the inequality of men and women in society, the proverbial wisdom of age turned on its head as the elders lie and the young Daniel exposes their sin and their crime both, the failure of the community, and the crucial willingness of the community to admit its wrong.

The two elders don't testify from any witness stand. Imagine this: As they testify, they "laid their hands on her head. Through her tears she looked up toward Heaven, for her heart trusted in the Lord" (vv. 34-35). The woman who has refused these two now must come before all while they put their hands on her head and tell lies about her. And that's it: the assembled neighbors believe the elders and condemn Susanna to die. Immediately.

That's when she makes the prayer above, though it isn't really a prayer at all, but a testimony. It is a cry, the story says, and the Lord hears and stirs up the spirit of the lad Daniel who confronts the lynch mob with this: "I want no part in shedding this woman's blood!" (v. 46). To their credit, they give him a hearing instead of scorn. Daniel seems fearless: "Are you such fools . . . as to condemn a daughter of Israel . . . without learning the facts? Return to court" (vv. 48-49). And they do, and they invite Daniel to ask the questions.

Why in Lent? What else do we know about an innocent person condemned to death? Susanna, for the church, foretells Jesus. And for us raises many questions of justice, of cowardice, of going along, of innocent people harmed and imprisoned and executed, of different standards for women and men. These are paschal questions.

> *Stir up in us, God of justice, the spirit that was in Daniel and the courage that was in Susanna so that we may challenge and question the stories of the powerful and be the helpers of the weak.*

TUESDAY, APRIL 8, 2003

What are human beings, that you make so much of them, that you set your mind on them, visit them every morning, test them every moment? Will you not look away from me for a while, let me alone until I swallow my spittle? JOB 7:17-19

CHAPTER 7 OF THE BOOK OF JOB is eloquent and devastating. A few reminders: "I am allotted months of emptiness, and nights of misery are apportioned to me. When I lie down I say, 'When shall I rise?' But the night is long, and I am full of tossing until dawn"(vv. 3-4). "My flesh is clothed with worms and dirt" (v. 5). "Those who go down to Sheol do not come up . . . nor do their places know them any more" (vv. 9-10). "You scare me with dreams and terrify me with visions, so that I would choose strangling and death rather than this body. I loathe my life" (vv. 14-16). "I shall lie in the earth; you will seek me, but I shall not be" (v. 21).

Elie Wiesel, writer about the Holocaust, retells the story of three rabbis. In the midst of terror and death inflicted on their Jewish communities, they meet one night in the concentration camp and bring charges against God for allowing these massacres. All night they make the case against God and at the end of this trial, they find God guilty. Then one of the rabbis realizes that it is near morning and says, "It is time for prayer!" And these three who have spent the night accusing and convicting God for allowing all the horrors of the Holocaust, bow their heads and begin the morning prayer.

How are we to understand these two, Job and the rabbis? The morning prayer the rabbis begin will be a prayer that praises God for creation and for God's fidelity and care. But there is no sign of any fidelity, any care. They see day by day the starvation, the disease, the misery, the hatred and meanness, the human spirit broken, the hard labor, the filth, the gas chambers.

What has Job said or what have the rabbis seen that we have not known also, not in our own flesh but before our eyes? The sufferings of our time in sheer numbers are greater than any before. The discipline of Lent is not simply to renew prayer in our lives, but to learn all its moments, to know there must be daily praise as there must be daily lament, and both of these come from the lips of those trying to find gospel lives in the world.

Strengthen us, dear God, to see what must be seen and to pray what we must pray. Teach us the whole vocabulary of the psalms and keep us faithful to the prayers of morning and night.

WEDNESDAY, APRIL 9, 2003

The hour has come for the Son of Man to be glorified. Very truly, I tell you, unless a grain of wheat falls into the earth and dies, it remains just a single grain; but if it dies, it bears much fruit.
JOHN 12:23-24

ON MARCH 24 WE THOUGHT ABOUT one such grain of wheat, Archbishop Oscar Romero, martyred in San Salvador in 1980 as he presided at Mass. Now on April 9 we remember another martyr. Pastor and theologian Dietrich Bonhoeffer was hanged by the Nazis on this day in 1945. He was one of thousands executed for their resistance just before the war ended. Though not yet 40, he had for ten years before his arrest in 1943 been a leader among those Lutherans in Germany who opposed both Hitler and the church's cooperation with Hitler. In his writing, as preacher and teacher, Bonhoeffer articulated a theology that allowed no room between gospel and life.

Because we as Americans and Christians opposed Hitler as did Bonhoeffer, we might think we can comfortably celebrate his life and work. Here is something he said that might give us a new perspective:

When a successful figure becomes especially prominent and conspicuous, the majority give way to the idolization of success. They become blind to right and wrong, truth and untruth, fair play and foul play. They have eyes only for the deed, for the successful result.

–*Ethics* (Simon & Schuster)

And here he speaks of being religious as not the same thing as being Christian: "It is not some religious act which makes a Christian, but participation in the suffering of God in the life of the world." And this, as we approach the end of Lent: "The figure of the Crucified invalidates all thought which takes success for its standard." This viewpoint must have helped him see that he must oppose even the churches when they would not oppose the government.

When Bonhoeffer said we had sold out the church for "cheap grace," he meant not only in the public and political realm, but even in our households. In *Life Together,* he wrote about the way Christians discipline their lives.

> We are silent at the beginning of the day because God should have the first word, and we are silent before going to sleep because the last word also belongs to God. . . . It is part of the discipline of humility that we must not spare our hand where it can perform a service and that we do not assume that our schedule is our own to manage, but allow it to be arranged by God.
>
> –*Life Together* (Harper Collins)

We give you thanks, O God, that you raise up in our midst the likes of Dietrich Bonhoeffer, that our church may be continually in reformation, continually in confrontation with all, however powerful, who bring harm to the weak, the poor, the earth itself.

THURSDAY, APRIL 10, 2003

The LORD hurled a great wind upon the sea, and such a mighty storm came . . . that the ship threatened to break up. The mariners . . . threw the cargo that was in the ship into the sea, to lighten it for them. Jonah, meanwhile, had gone down into the hold of the ship and had laid down, and was fast asleep. JONAH 1:4-5

THE BOOK OF JONAH, a marvelous tale, is read by some churches at the Vigil of Easter. Here we are at the beginning. God has told Jonah to go east and preach to Nineveh. Jonah has gone west and has boarded a ship to get him as far west as one could go. God takes up the challenge and sends a storm. Where's Jonah? Elie Wiesel asks the question this way:

> The wind is howling, the waves are roaring, the ship is about to break up into a thousand pieces; everybody is busy, everybody tries to help; some work, others pray. . . . Everybody is trying to be useful except Jonah. What is his contribution to the collective rescue operation? Incredible but true: In that hour of crisis and mortal danger, when the world is upside down, when creation is in turmoil, the prophet—who should, by definition, be more sensitive, more alert, more tense than the common mortal—is asleep!
>
> *–Five Biblical Portraits* (University of Notre Dame Press)

Who could sleep through such a time? Jonah could. The mariners tell him to pray, ask what god he worships, and when they realize that Jonah is fleeing his God, they know why the storm has come. Jonah, to his credit, says: "Throw me into the sea and save yourselves." But they don't want to. They try everything first and then they cry out: "O Lord, do not make us guilty of innocent blood!" And in he goes. The storm is over. You have to love these mariners, and you have to wonder why God would choose anyone like this Jonah. The question becomes even sharper when the story concludes a few pages further on.

Even late in Lent we can ask: Where is this ship headed and how and why did we get on board? And how sound asleep are we? It is a question we will hear Jesus ask some heavy-eyed disciples in Gethsemane.

> *You, Lord, cast me into the deep, into the heart of the seas, and the flood surrounded me; all your waves and your billows passed over me. (from Jonah 2:3)*

FRIDAY, APRIL 11, 2003

> *[Nebuchadnezzar] ordered the furnace heated up seven times more than was customary, and ordered some of the strongest guards in his army to bind Shadrach, Meshach, and Abednego and to throw them into the furnace of blazing fire.*
> DANIEL 3:19-20

Where do the Shadrachs, Meshachs, and Abednegos of the world come from? When millions of Germans and Austrians took up arms under Hitler's orders, where did Franz Jägerstätter come from? A young man from a peasant background, Franz had only his wife—soon to be a widow—standing by him during prison and execution. Yet he had the courage to say "No" to serving in Hitler's army. Where do those who stand in front of a tank, alone, come from?

A family of seven brothers and their mother, as 2 Maccabees 7 tells it, were arrested and threatened with torture and death unless they ate pork. Most of the Jews found it very possible to go along with the new rulers and still keep their religion. Not this family. One by one they were put to death. A young man put out his hands to the torturers and said: "I got these from Heaven, and because of his laws I disdain them, and from him I hope to get them back again" (v. 11). Where do such people come from? And amazingly the litany goes on, from many lands—those who say, "Enough!" in a hundred languages. Some few we know about; most are lost to memory.

Shadrach could have made a little bow and gone on supporting his family. Why not? Why make them suffer for his fanaticism? And that is a right question and needs an answer. Most of us decide to pay our taxes next week. Certainly we know that these dollars will be used for many good things and some evil things. But we pay. We bow. We eat the forbidden food. We drop a little incense on the coals. Nothing's perfect, we say, and at least it does some good for some folks. There are enough fanatics in the world.

Perhaps because it is difficult to make the judgments, let alone follow through with deeds that risk humiliation and punishment, we need the church. We need in our assemblies great and small to confront and struggle with the hard questions.

> We honor the martyrs, O God, but we know little
> of their courage, less of their certainty. Bring our
> church to the hard questions and help us listen to
> your word and to one another.

SATURDAY, APRIL 12, 2003

I will meditate on your precepts, and fix my eyes on your ways. I will delight in your statutes; I will not forget your word. PSALM 119:15-16

So WE STAND BEFORE the last five days of Lent. Lent ends when evening comes on Maundy (or Holy) Thursday. We leave behind this season of penance and preparation and we enter the Holy Triduum, the Paschal Three Days. From Thursday night until Easter Sunday evening we are at the core of our year. We ponder, proclaim, experience in our bodies and spirits and community the passover of our Lord and our own passover in Christ.

Are we ready? Probably not, but we have five days. In his Easter sermon that is still read each year in some churches, John Chrysostom (died 407) said: "Come you all and enter into the joy of your Lord. You the first and you the last, you sober and you weaklings, you who have kept the fast and you who have not, rejoice today!" So if we have been keeping Lent steadily with prayer and fasting and almsgiving, we can hang on for these five days. If we have forgotten, then we can seize these five days for our intense preparation for the Triduum. It is not about self-improvement, after all, but about building up the body of Christ.

So if we have not yet fasted from distractions, we can begin today. Distractions are all the ways we stuff our time full: the needless running around, the constant switching on of entertainment devices, the chatting on the phone in all places and times. Whatever it is that prevents us from "fixing our eyes on your ways" as the psalm says, put it aside these days. Fast from food also. Put aside all but the basic eating that we need to do. Live on a Third World diet. We put aside anger and impatience. We take whatever we can of prayer and scripture reading and the like. The point is not to punish oneself. The point is to free ourselves to be Christ's.

And if our almsgiving has been sporadic so far in Lent, we take a look around at what we do with our possessions, our money, our time, our energy. Maybe we can't make a significant change in these five days, but we can ponder all this. Again, the point is to free ourselves to belong to Christ.

Tomorrow we take the palms and sing "Hosanna!" It is a wild sort of moment, but most of us act timidly. Think what is going on here as branches and flowers adorn the church—that is, not the building, but us, the church. All of this Lent-keeping, this work of fasting and alms, we have not done alone. We have done it together. Maybe I did a lot, maybe a little, but the church was doing it together. And now, together, we walk into this holy week proclaiming a great mystery.

> *Open to me the gates of righteousness, Lord, that I may enter through them and give you thanks. I thank you that you have answered me and have become my salvation. (from Psalm 118:19, 21)*

SUNDAY OF THE PASSION, APRIL 13, 2003

> *[Christ] became obedient to the point of death— even death on a cross. Therefore God also highly exalted him and gave him the name that is above every name.* PHILIPPIANS 2:8-9

IN HIS LETTER TO THE CHURCH at Philippi, Paul writes out what was probably even then a familiar song about how Christ poured himself out—obedient even to death on the cross—and that God has exalted Christ, and we proclaim that Jesus Christ is Lord to the glory of God the Father. Philippians 2:5-11 is a magnificent statement of the Christian faith, one we might well know by heart. Paul then goes on to many things, some of them quite practical about journeys and so on, but he never quits thinking about this song.

> I regard everything as loss because of the surpassing value of knowing Christ Jesus my Lord. For his sake I have suf- fered the loss of all things, and I regard them as rubbish, in order that I may gain Christ and be found in him. . . . I want to know Christ and the power of his resurrection and the sharing of his sufferings by becoming like him in his death, if somehow I may attain the resurrection from the

dead. . . . I press on to make it my own, because Christ Jesus has made me his own.

–Phil. 3:8-12

"Like Christ in his death. Attain the resurrection. I press on." All this is for us this week. We hear today the Passion proclaimed and set our faces toward Lent's end and the Triduum. But Paul is clear: we're not just individuals making more, or less, heroic efforts. We are the church, a not-so-glorious assembly of sinful and often irritating human beings. But we are the church! Who is now to empty themselves, who is to confront even death, who is to embrace the cross? Whether baptized last year or decades and decades past, this week with the strength of the church we too can say: "I have suffered the loss of all things and I regard them as rubbish. I want to know Christ and the power of his resurrection—and the sharing of his sufferings by becoming like him in his death." That's what the church timidly rehearses today as we prepare for the Three Days when Lent has ended.

> Stir up your church, O Lord, that we may embrace these days without fear and seek in them the truth that we must proclaim with our lives given in love for the world.

MONDAY, APRIL 14, 2003

> Their mouths are filled with cursing and deceit and oppression; under their tongues are mischief and iniquity. They sit in ambush in the villages; in hiding places they murder the innocent.
> PSALM 10:7-8

THESE PSALMS OF SUFFERING, of seeing wrong done, of anger at God, are part of our vocabulary. So often we favor the pretty and positive psalm verses and hymns, but that's not the whole of our biblical language. We need this other. Psalm 10 helps. It gives us language to get angry and to get going, language to stand before God and say, "Why do you hide yourself in times of trouble?" Then this psalm helps us to name the troubles: the everlasting suffering of the poor at the hands of the wealthy, the arrogance of the powerful, the careless killing of the innocent, the striking of terror in people's hearts.

It was in such a mind that the bishop of San Salvador, Oscar Romero, preached to rich and poor more than 20 years ago:

For the church, the many abuses of human life, liberty and dignity are a heartfelt suffering. The church, entrusted with the earth's glory, believes that in each person is the Creator's image and that everyone who tramples it offends God. As the holy defender of God's right and of God's images, the church must cry out. It takes as spittle in its face, as lashes on its back, as the cross in its passion, all that human beings suffer, even though they be unbelievers. They suffer as God's images. There is no dichotomy between humans and God's image. Whoever tortures a human being, whoever abuses a human being, whoever outrages a human being abuses God's image, and the church takes as its own that cross, that martyrdom.

–Sermon, Dec. 31, 1977

This is the bold vocabulary of the psalmist. If what Romero says is so, how would one recognize "the church"? It seems the church he is describing would look like Jesus in the passion: spit and thorns and blood and abuse. The image of God is being trampled in these times, and the church will stand with those abused. But also, he says, "The church must cry out." How and what and to whom shall we cry out? How can we understand that such crying out is not something the church does, but something the church is?

> O LORD, *you will hear the desire of the meek; you will strengthen their heart, you will incline your ear to do justice for the orphan and the oppressed, so that those from earth may strike terror no more. (Psalm 10:17-18)*

TUESDAY, APRIL 15, 2003

*Rouse yourself! Why do you sleep, O Lord?
Awake, do not cast us off forever! Why do you
hide your face? Why do you forget our affliction
and oppression?* PSALM 44:23-24

THE LESSONS IN THE VOCABULARY of prayer continue. Yesterday we read Psalm 10, today we read Psalm 44. When we strive for some language to speak of God, to speak to God also, we have the psalms to be our teachers as they were the teachers of Mary, of Jesus, of Paul. But it seems we seldom get the harsher stuff into our mouths. That is too bad, for such a language can order God: "Rouse yourself!" and can challenge God: "Why do you sleep?" and can say what seems so obvious: "Why do you forget?"

It is deep in us to intercede before God. We do this when we assemble on the Lord's day in the various petitions that we make, sometimes prepared, sometimes spontaneous, almost always with the whole assembly joining in a refrain ("Lord, have mercy" or "Lord, hear our prayer" are examples). And we probably do this also in our household or personal praying each day: lifting up to God the names of people who are sick, of our family and friends, of those who have died, of the present sadness and terror in the world.

At one point in the life of the church, many centuries ago, the public prayers of intercession were understood as part of the very identity of the baptized Christian. Those who were preparing for baptism through the lengthy catechumenate were not allowed to remain with those already baptized for these prayers (or for the peace greeting, or for the eucharist). Some deeds one could not do until after baptism. For those baptized, then, to intercede with God was both a right and a duty. It was privilege and obligation, as if to say: Now that you have died and live as the body of Christ, you must do what Christ does. You must be a voice calling out to God— who might be asleep, who might forget—about all the harm, all the trouble, all the evil that fills this world. You are baptized to be the voice of all the world. Open your eyes, look around, take it all in. Clamor before God! And here, to be your teacher, is this amazing book of psalms.

> *We sink down to the dust; our bodies cling to the ground. Rise up, O Lord, come to our help. Redeem us for the sake of your steadfast love. (from Psalm 44:25-26)*

WEDNESDAY, APRIL 16, 2003

> *As [Jesus] sat at the table, a woman came with an alabaster jar of very costly ointment of nard, and she broke open the jar and poured the ointment on his head.* MARK 14:3

THIS STORY OF THE WOMAN who anointed Jesus for burial is the true prologue to the telling of the passion, death, and resurrection of Jesus. All four evangelists tell it, though in different ways (see Mark 14:3-9 and John 12:1-8). We can ponder the following aspects of Mark's telling of the story.

The woman enters an assembly of men, uninvited. Here and in other places Jesus invites or welcomes deeds that upset the prejudices of the accepted ways. Such a deed—one not done at Jesus' invitation—comes now at the climax of his ministry.

She carries a fine vessel, which she breaks open. There is a "pouring out" like that which Jesus himself is doing. Both the vessel and contents are precious; the action of breaking accentuates the urgency of her deed. John's gospel says that the "house was filled with the fragrance of the perfume"; we think of how just a few verses earlier John writes of Martha saying that there is already a stench because Lazarus has been dead four days. And one thinks too of how Paul calls Christians to be the fragrance of Christ in 2 Corinthians 2:14.

Luke and John tell of anointing Jesus' feet (for John, perhaps a preparation for what Jesus will do for the disciples at the last supper), but Mark (and Matthew follows) say she anointed Jesus' head. In any case, Jesus says clearly what this woman's deed is all about. He calls what she has done "a good service," and says, "She has done what she could" and she has "anointed my body beforehand for its burial" (v. 8). As usual, the disciples present don't seem to get it.

This will be told everywhere "in remembrance of her" (v. 9). Her? But we don't even know her name. And we remember the line about the poor more than any other part of the story. Time to change that. Time to remember her! Time to know the compassion and the beauty and the lavishness and the boldness of what she showed us about the deeds of one who has received the gospel.

> Be in our midst, O God, as the days of Lent come
> to an end tomorrow, and draw us into the Three
> Days where we celebrate the paschal mystery, the
> death and resurrection of the Lord Jesus Christ.

THURSDAY, APRIL 17, 2003

*Jesus answered, "Unless I wash you, you have no
share with me." Simon Peter said to him, "Lord,
not my feet only but also my hands and my
head!"* JOHN 13:8-9

TONIGHT WE LEAVE LENT BEHIND and enter the Three Days, the Paschal Triduum. Thursday night to Sunday evening is the heart of our year, a time to abandon work, food, entertainment, distraction, and live first in anticipation and then in celebration of what happens in our midst at the Easter Vigil.

But tonight we enter with the washing of feet. If a foot-washing ritual is included in our assembly's worship, it is not done to play-act what Jesus did at the last supper. Nothing of these days is play-acting. It is all to be the real world. We take this deed told of by John's gospel. Alone, John tells us nothing of bread and wine at the last supper—that was addressed in chapter 6 and elsewhere. Instead, John tells us of this washing of feet. From the snatch of conversation with Peter, above, we know it wasn't all that different then than it is now.

If we find ourselves having our feet washed tonight, and washing the feet of others, it is so we can enter these days not simply recalling what was long ago and far away, but to enter into what is here, now, the gospel life into which we were baptized and into which we now, on the night between Saturday and Sunday, baptize others. What kind of a world do we proclaim as we kneel and wash feet and dry and kiss them? If we let that world stay inside our church hall, something went wrong. Jesus himself walked outside, got arrested and executed in short order. To tell the truth, it was for washing feet. So what we do to get ourselves out of Lent and into the Three Days is a gesture that proclaims what kind of world we mean to be.

So enter a time like no other in the year. Be with the assembly whenever it gathers, but keep all the other hours too as vigil and prayer and eager anticipation. Here is what an unknown early poet said of this Pasch, this Passover, this blessed time: "The Pasch breathes balm, is great, was made for the faithful; the Pasch opens to us the gates of paradise. O Pasch, sanctify all believers."

> *We thank you, God, for bringing this church through the days of Lent. Be with us now as we keep the Pasch, clinging to the cross of our Lord Jesus Christ.*

THE THREE DAYS

GOOD FRIDAY, APRIL 18, 2003

> *So they took Jesus; and carrying the cross by himself, he went out to what is called The Place of the Skull, which in Hebrew is called Golgotha.*
> JOHN 19:17

THIS IS THE FIRST OF THE THREE DAYS, though according to the church's reckoning, it began last night. On this day we keep from work. We fast, read the scriptures, gather with the assembly to listen to the Passion proclaimed and to venerate the holy cross.

The cross—perhaps invisible to us because so multiplied— is in our tradition a wondrous image, at once the instrument of execution and the throne of the victorious Christ. It is the tree of Paradise that undid Eve and Adam, the ark that saved humanity, the wood Isaac carried, the ladder Jacob saw reaching to heaven, the staff of Moses, the vine that grows to embrace the world. Artists have often made it more a picture (a crucifix) than an image, placing Christ dying or dead or even risen upon the cross. But the church mostly clings to the image itself, whether it be the "old rugged cross" or the jeweled cross of medieval cathedrals.

And why should this be? Litanies have been written and prayed that name the cross in many ways. Door of Paradise. Foundation of the faithful. Protection guarding the church. Invincible weapon. Adversary of demons. Glory of martyrs. True beauty of saints. Haven of salvation. Guide to the blind. Healer of the sick. Resurrection of the dead.

An ancient refrain goes: "We worship you, Lord. We venerate your cross. We praise your resurrection. Through the cross you brought joy to the world." Stop and be amazed: Cross and joy cast together. How does that affect the way we live?

If it is our custom to mark our bodies with the cross when we pray, or when we arise in the morning or retire at night, then here all these images are gathered and marked on our own bodies. What we are doing is at once a clinging to the cross, our place of safety and solace, and a reminding: This is the saving shape of our lives and day-by-day and night-by-night we will put it on until in fact we have made it ours.

> Dear God, in paradise of old the wood stripped us bare. Now the wood of the cross clothes us with the garment of life, and the whole world is filled with boundless joy.
> (from the Orthodox liturgy)

HOLY SATURDAY, APRIL 19, 2003

I will both lie down and sleep in peace; for you alone, O LORD, make me lie down in safety.
PSALM 4:8

THE FASTING OF ANTICIPATION CONTINUES—from work, from food, from diversions. It is the blessed sabbath when God rested, when Christ rested. We rest also and await the night when in the darkness the church assembles to keep vigil and to read one scripture after another, unfolding the whole story, so that we might know what it is we are doing when we approach the font and baptize those who have long prepared for this night.

There is an ancient homily for this day that the church still reads. It tells of "something strange, a great silence on earth and stillness." Why? Because God has fallen asleep in the flesh. And because hell trembles with fear.

The homily then images what happens this day: Christ who has died goes in search of Adam and Eve and all the others. He shatters hell's gates and says to all: "Awake, O sleeper, and rise from the dead." And Christ takes Eve and Adam by the hand and speaks to them of what has happened—to them and to him:

For the sake of you who left a garden, I was betrayed in a garden and crucified in a garden. See on my face the spittle I received in order to restore to you the life I once breathed into you. See there the marks of the blows I received in order to refashion your warped nature in my image. On my back see the marks of the scourging I endured to remove the burden of sin that weighs upon your back. See my hands, nailed firmly to a tree, for you who once wickedly stretched out your hand to a tree. I slept on the cross and a sword pierced my side for you who slept in paradise and brought forth Eve from your side. My side has healed the pain in yours. My sleep will rouse you from your sleep in hell. The sword that pierced me has sheathed the sword that was turned against you. Rise, the bridal chamber is adorned, the banquet is ready, the kingdom of heaven has been prepared for you from all eternity.

–from an ancient homily, Office of Readings, Holy Saturday, Roman rite. Quoted in *A Triduum Sourcebook* (Liturgy Training Publications).

All these parallels may seem a little strange to us, but ponder them. And remember, it isn't about Adam and Eve. It's about us, this Holy Saturday.

> O Lord, by your burial you have opened for me a
> door to life, and by your death you have brought
> an end to death and hell. (Prayer from the Orthodox liturgy)

EASTER SUNDAY, APRIL 20, 2003

> Tremble, O earth, at the presence of the LORD, at
> the presence of the God of Jacob, who turns the
> rock into a pool of water, the flint into a spring of
> water.   PSALM 114:7-8

TREMBLE, O EARTH! The third of the Three Days is the first of the Fifty Days, the season of Easter that will be counted all the way to Pentecost. The rock has become a pool of water, the flint a spring of water. Those newly baptized and smeared with fragrant oil have come with us at last to the table and we have thanked God over the gifts of bread and wine and have tasted the goodness of the Lord. We have, in fact, glimpsed that our proclamation of Christ's death and resurrection is a proclamation of the struggle the baptized enter from now on.

Here is something both beautiful and fun. It is a paragraph of an Easter homily from fourteenth-century England with most of the spelling kept as it was. A good homily then, a good homily now.

This day is also callyd Pase-day, that is in Englysch, the passyng day. . . . Ych Godys chyld shall passe out of evell lyvyng into good lyvyng, out of vyccs, ynto vertuys, out of pride ynto mekenes, out of covetyse ynto largenes, out of sloth ynto holy bysynes, out of envy ynto love and charite, out of wrathe ynto mercy, out of gloteny ynto abstynens, out of lechery ynto chastyte, out of the fendys clochus [fiends' clutches] ynto Godys barm [bosom]; and soo of Godys enmy make Godys frende and derlyng. Whosoe passythe thus, is worthy forto come to that gret fest that God makythe thys day to all that thys passage makut.

We have holy bysynes before us, best get at it. We have passed over. In Christ. And what a passing it has been, and is, and will be. Because we are delivered from the "fendys clochus," and no longer "Godys enmy" we are "Godys frende" and even more, in the dearest words of this passage, we are "Godys derlyng." That was what Lent was all about. And now we shall live as God's darling these Fifty Days of Easter. And on. Forever.

> *Blessed are you, Lord God of all creation, in the passing over of our Lord Jesus Christ, and in Christ our passing over. As your friends, your darlings, show us the way that brings life to all your children.*